SEPARATED AT BIRTH?

2

THE SAGA CONTINUES

SEPARATED

A Dolphin Book
Doubleday

New York London Toronto Sydney Auckland

AT BIRTH?

2

by the
Editors of
SPY

THE SAGA CONTINUES

Picture editors Nicki Gostin
Ted Heller
Design B. W. Honeycutt
Type and layout Joe Mastrianni
Picture research Giulia Melucci
Julie Mihaly
Ty Robertson
Interns Jarvis E.D. Murphy
Leslie Chang

A Dolphin Book
PUBLISHED BY DOUBLEDAY
A division of Bantam Doubleday Dell Publishing Group, Inc.
666 Fifth Avenue, New York, New York 10103
DOLPHIN, DOUBLEDAY, and the portrayal of two dolphins are trademarks of
Doubleday, a division of Bantam Doubleday Dell Publishing Group, Inc.

Library of Congress Cataloging-in-Publication data
Separated at birth? 2 : the saga continues / by the editors of Spy . – 1st ed.
p. 128   21 x 14 cm.
"A Dolphin book"
ISBN 0-385-41099-9
1. Lookalikes–Humor. 2. Celebrities–Humor. 3. American wit and humor
I Spy (New York, N.Y.) II Title: Separated at birth? Two.
PN6231.L58S48   1990
920.02--dc20   89-71443
CIP

CONTENTS

Since the publication of our first *Separated at Birth?* book in November 1988, SPY magazine has infiltrated Henry Kissinger and Ronald Reagan's summer camp, produced a television special, offered a guided tour of atrocities committed at Harry and Leona Helmsley's Connecticut home, dropped a Twinkie from nine stories up, celebrated America's stupidest legislators, gone wildlife slaughtering with John and Pat Kluge, published a parody of Cliffs Notes, won an important federal case regarding parodies of Cliffs Notes, made it impossible for our research department to

HERE WE GO AGAIN

Son of SEPARATED AT BIRTH?

ever again get any assistance whatsoever from the Museum of Broadcasting, mounted a SoHo art exhibit of talented young painters of the 1980s (okay, talented young painters who were *born* in the 1980s), sponsored and judged the Second Annual Celebrity Pro-Am Ironman Nightlife Decathlon, turned New York's mayoral race into a board game, picked through famous people's garbage, commemorated the Cold War in stirring words and pictures, talked Elvis Costello into wearing small curved horns for our cover, made appointments with expensive, famous quacks (and kept them), gone to

Washington with a vengeance, visited the Los Angeles Friars Club, taken an appreciative look at the 1970s, seriously considered cryonics and time travel, corresponded with Donald Trump, distilled four David Mamet plays down to seven riveting minutes of theater and then produced them onstage using Mamet's own ensemble, dug up the only existing copy of our November 1964 debut issue and reprinted it, diapered a baby with the American flag (it was urgent) and cured thousands of people of the air-quote habit.

All of which, naturally, has led us to another book of photos of people who look alike.

We don't mean to sound bitter. It's not that we have anything against quality paperback sequels to quality paperback best-sellers. It's not that we aren't flattered when Jay Leno asks us to put together a few astonishing pairs for one or another of his delightful *Tonight Show* appearances. It's not that we aren't somehow pleased that readers still flood our offices with good and bad *Separated at Birth?* suggestions or corner us at parties with the same. And it's not that we don't want to try to satisfy an insatiable public that apparently demands a steady diet of look-alikes.

It's just that—well, never mind. We will say this: cheap, popular entertainment doesn't come any more scrupulously or lovingly assembled than this.

In *Separated at Birth? 2: The Saga Continues*, the basic comic premise remains the same as it did in the first book: A resembles B, and sometimes C. (The speculation in intellectual circles that we got the idea for *Separated at Birth?* from Max Eastman's *The Enjoyment of Laughter* is true only in the most superficial sense. Our copy of Eastman's work happens to sit on the shelf right next to Peter Ueberroth's autobiography. Both are massive hardcovers, with blue, uncracked spines. *Ping!* From there it was an easy leap to matching King Hussein with G. Gordon Liddy.)

But this time around we're more fiercely motivated than ever by a desire to break new ground in the burgeoning resonant-look-alike field. So *Separated at Birth? 2* contains—in addition to the thematic chapters, the triplets, the cross-species pairs and the cartoon-human combinations pioneered in the first volume—some innovations that just might revolutionize the entire "Resemblicant" industry.

Such as *Separated at the Easel*. A life-imitates-art phenomenon, first isolated and tested scientifically in a March 1989 SPY feature—a feature that proved, among other things, that Cher is an Aubrey Beardsley drawing come to narcissistic life.

More innovations are anticipated in time for *Separated at Birth? 3* (you may have noticed that the subtitle of this book is *The Saga Continues*, not *The Final Chapter*). Even now, top-secret research is being conducted at the SPY Laboratories, out beyond the coffee machine. We won't say anything more than this: if "Project JE6: *Separated at Ethos*" is successful, someday in the not-too-distant future two individuals' actual guiding beliefs will be displayed side by side and found to be virtually indistinguishable . . . *to comic effect!*

We don't need to suggest the ramifications of *that.*

But back to the current sequel. How did we

put it together? Assembling really gratifying combinations is still pretty simple: Someone notices that someone looks like someone else, scores of photos are gathered, and if any resulting pair scores high on the incongruous resemblance meter—*voilà!* Only the idolatrous caption remains to be written. As to why the average SPY look-alike tends to work better than the average uncredited ripoff look-alike perpetrated by, say, unimaginative columnists in the pages of midwestern newspapers—well, the way we run the photos—cropped to the same size, side by side, the subjects facing the same way, perhaps with similar expressions or gestures—doesn't hurt.

So here are David Byrne and Mister Rogers, Peggy Lee and Joan Kennedy, Bette Davis and the Mean Apple Tree from *The Wizard of Oz*, Mary McFadden and William Shakespeare, Salman Rushdie and Mick Fleetwood, Imelda Marcos and Diane Sawyer, and, yes, Prince and Cantinflas, all doing what they do best: reminding you intriguingly of someone else.

We hope we enjoy *Separated at Birth? 2: The Saga Continues* as much as you will.

—*The Editors*

ave we got a package for you! A multigenerational epic with young Peter Ueberroth growing up to be Leonard Cohen! *No, wait!* Make it a small, bittersweet slice-of-life film about two con men—I see Bob Guccione and Naguib Mahfouz above the marquee! Whatever, *it's a guaranteed blockbuster!*

Great, spacey actor John Malkovich. . .

and great, spacey actress Amanda Plummer?

Actor-of-his-generation Marlon Brando . . .

and actor-of-his-generation Orson Welles's Charles Foster Kane?

Scary, cool actor
Jack Nicholson . . .

and scary, cool Nobel literature
laureate Naguib Mahfouz?

Leading man
Harrison Ford . . .

and folksy yarn-spinner
Will Rogers?

Quasi-career-coaster
John Candy . . .

and Quasimodo portrayer
Charles Laughton?

1970s sex phenomenon
Richard Gere . . .

and 1970s est phenomenon
Werner Erhard?

Cheery, child-loving UNICEF spokesman Danny Kaye . . .

and reclusive, child-loving *Eloise* creator Kay Thompson?

Talented egomaniac Dustin Hoffman . . .

and not-so-talented singer-poet Leonard Cohen?

13

Comeback star Al Pacino . . .

and cuddly Scottish nonstar Tom Conti?

Elegant, gravelly-voiced actor Michael Douglas . . .

and elegant, gravelly-voiced Actors' Equity dowager Colleen Dewhurst?

Big star Tom Hanks . . .

and onetime big star
Tony Curtis?

Crowd-pleaser Bill Murray . . .

and crowd-pleaser
Edgar Allan Poe?

Teen substance abuser
Drew Barrymore . . .

and Bowery Boy Leo Gorcey?

Overrated pin-up
Daryl Hannah . . .

and underrated composer
Todd Rundgren?

Broody erotic pioneer Montgomery Clift . . .

and broody atomic pioneer Robert Oppenheimer?

Fleshy workaholic Michael Caine . . .

and fleshy sexaholic Bob Guccione Sr.?

Show biz revivalist Tommy Tune . . .

and show biz remnant Farley Granger?

Preternaturally squeaky-clean Michael J. Fox . . .

and posturing moralizer Peter Ueberroth?

elevision's sexiest show is also television's most lawyerly show. Hey, who wouldn't be turned on by a French smoothie, a mass-murderer, and Daniel Boone's Indian sidekick? And isn't that Alex Keaton's dad presiding over the case?

Mellow TV dad Michael Gross . . .

and mellow pothead judge Douglas Ginsburg?

Jimmy Smits as himself . . .

and Ed Ames as Mingo?

***L.A. Law*'s Alan Rachins . . .**

and Louis Jourdan?

***L.A. Law* litigator
Harry Hamlin . . .**

**and L.A. Night Stalker
Richard Ramirez?**

***Head of the Class* actor
Brian Robbins . . .**

**and Ali McGraw of tomorrow
Jami Gertz?**

Second-banana-made-good Regis Philbin . . .

and banana-hammock-wearing Olympic diver Greg Louganis?

Immigrant-portrayer Bronson Pinchot . . .

and immigrant-welcomer Emma Lazarus?

Midnight Caller's **Gary Cole . . .**

and actor Kevin Bacon?

Perspiring Canadian William Shatner . . .

and dry wit John Larroquette?

Cabbage Patch thespian Tina Yothers . . .

and husky bluester Bonnie Raitt?

Wealth accumulator Bill Cosby . . .

and jazz drummer Max Roach?

Bulbous actor Robert (*Batman*) Wuhl. . .

and post-pubescent actor Kirk (*Growing Pains*) Cameron?

Putative actress Donna Mills . . .

and putative musician Linda McCartney?

Cheers's Kirstie Alley . . .

and actress Meg Foster?

Former Nancy Reagan pal Mike Wallace . . .

and former Nancy Reagan pal Diana Vreeland?

n which Diana Vreeland becomes a hard-hitting investigative reporter.

Overpaid fetish object Diane Sawyer . . .

and overindulged widow Imelda Marcos?

High-strung anchorguy Dan Rather . . .

and low-wattage Senator Charles Robb?

Tom Brokaw . . .

and Louisville University basketball coach Denny Crum?

Impeccable poet W. H. Aden . . .

and impeccable newscaster Robert MacNeil?

Bryant Gumbel . . .

and classical pianist
André Watts?

Newscaster Pat Harper . . .

and denture wearer
Martha Raye?

NBC News's Jane Pauley . . .

and *Bewitched* star
Elizabeth Montgomery?

U.S. Commerce Secretary Bob
"Mr. Georgette" Mosbacher . . .

and television sensationalist
Maury "Mr. Chung" Povich?

ABC News correspondent
Barry Serafin . . .

and Inspector Clouseau victim
Herbert Lom?

ABC reporter Lynn Sherr . . .

and "Come On a My House"
singer Rosemary Clooney?

People who are paid lots of money to encourage other,
generally more accomplished people to set up the clip.

Beloved national treasure Jay Leno . . .

and treasure-chest-shaped Kaye Ballard?

Johnny Carson . . .

and Tommy Smothers?

Steve "Without Jayne I'm Nothing" Allen . . .

and Randy "Without Dennis I'm Nothing" Quaid?

Connecticut-based former talk show host Jack Paar . . .

and Connecticut-based perfume endorser Bill Blass?

Kitsch king Joe Franklin . . .

and the guy on Portuguese currency?

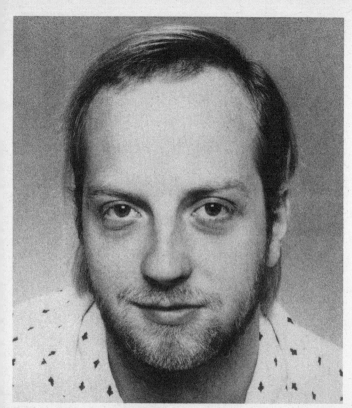

29

Bob and Ray's son, Chris Elliott . . .

and father figure of Broadway, Hal Prince?

N

Manic comedian
Jackie Gleason . . .

and *Mannix* actor
Mike Connors?

**ow playing in syndicated reruns
at a local station near you.**

Mannered-but-lovable Robert De Niro . . .

and daddy to millions Danny Thomas?

Composer Leonard Bernstein . . .

and composer's son Efrem Zimbalist Jr.?

Richard (*Götterdämmerung*) Wagner . . .

and John (*Bizarre*) Byner?

Desert dweller Georgia O'Keeffe . . .

and Sanka pitchman Robert Young?

W

Sick-joke-maker
Milton Berle . . .

and sick-joke-topic
Helen Keller?

ho says there's nothing
funny about Helen Keller?

Philharmonic conductor Zubin Mehta . . .

and sophomoric comedian Howie Mandel?

Wiggy actor-author
Peter Ustinov . . .

and card-carrying Whig
Millard Fillmore?

Too-thin 1960s artifact
Dick Gregory . . .

and toothless 1960s artifact
Richie Havens?

Swiss playwright
Friedrich Dürrenmatt . . .

and singer-songwriter Allan
"Hello Mudduh, Hello
Fadduh!" Sherman?

Talky comedian Jackie Mason . . .

and tacky clothier Bijan?

Bespectacled eggheady poet Robert Lowell . . .

and bespectacled eggheady jokester Buck Henry . . .

and bespectacled eggheady WKRP newsreader Les Nessman?

Georgia senator
Sam Nunn . . .

and actor Chevy Chase?

t's a hawkish senator from
Georgia, a washed-up clothier
and a onetime drug addict!

Phil Hartman . . .

and career-dead Halston?

Pissy, self-satisfied comic
Dennis Miller . . .

and pouty, self-satisfied actor
Gabriel Byrne?

Pumped-up has-been
Joe Piscopo . . .

and cool-guy survivor
Lou Reed?

Pathological liar Jon Lovitz . . .

and pathological Hollywood
spender Michael
(*Heaven's Gate*) Cimino?

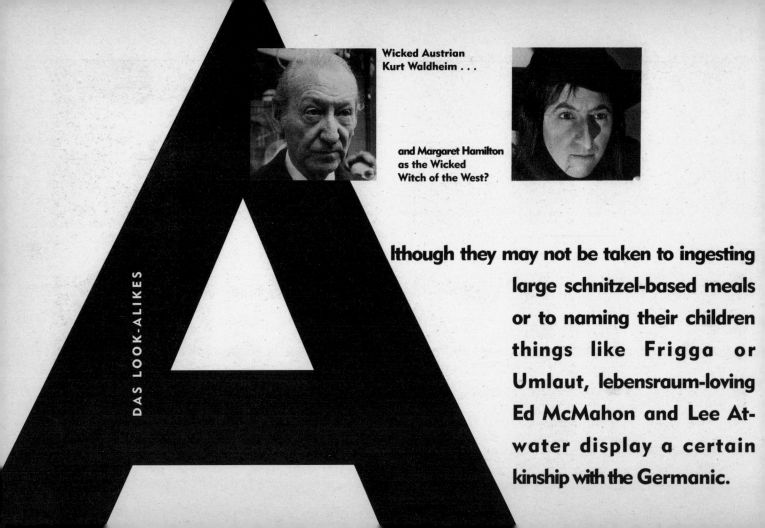

Wicked Austrian
Kurt Waldheim . . .

and Margaret Hamilton
as the Wicked
Witch of the West?

Although they may not be taken to ingesting large schnitzel-based meals or to naming their children things like Frigga or Umlaut, lebensraum-loving Ed McMahon and Lee Atwater display a certain kinship with the Germanic.

Duke University basketball coach Mike Krzyzewski . . .

and Adolf Hitler?

Adolf Hitler honey Eva Braun . . .

and Jimmy Stewart honey Jean Arthur?

Filmmaker Garry Marshall . . .

and former East German leader Egon Krenz?

West German Chancellor Helmut Kohl . . .

and direct mail mascot Ed McMahon?

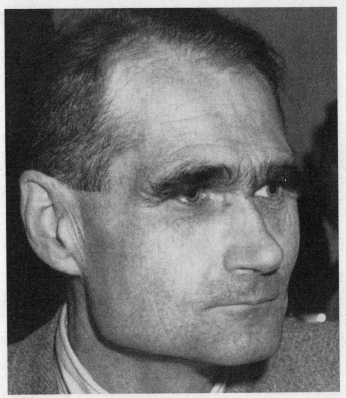

Republican propagandist Lee Atwater . . .

and *Mein Kampf* amanuensis Rudolf Hess?

Nazi propagandist Hermann Göring . . .

and Emmy shoo-in *L.A. Law*'s Larry Drake?

Human oddity
Brigitte Nielsen . . .

and perpetual survivor
Joey Heatherton?

The Male Animal's
Henry Fonda . . .

and male animal Rob Lowe?

Pajama-clad pornographer
Hugh Hefner . . .

and former *What's My Line*
sensation Orson Bean?

Bloated yenta Shelley Winters . . .

and Michelin-Man-like socialite
Bubbles Rothermere?

Anomalies. Miscreations. People for whom the circus is more than just a place to take the kids on a Sunday afternoon.

FREAKS

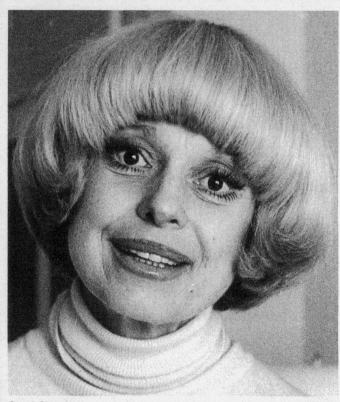

Carol Channing . . .

and Señor Wences's hand?

Judge Robert Bork . . .

and Tom Thumb?

Britain's Gidget, Helena Bonham Carter . . .

and Barnum's midget, Mrs. Tom Thumb?

Heterosexual choreographer Peter Martins . . .

and Bond nemesis Richard "Jaws" Kiel?

Frightening soul sister Patti LaBelle . . .

and the Bride of Frankenstein?

Bozo Geraldo Rivera . . .

and Bozo the Clown?

47

P

Late-1950s sensation Bobby Darin . . .

and early-1960s sensation Lee Harvey Oswald?

eople who look like (in some cases alleged) killers: life's unwitting walking mug shots.

Heartthrobby hockey star Wayne Gretzky . . .

and heartless murderer Nathan Leopold?

Forgotten Brat Packer Andrew McCarthy . . .

and 1920s murderer Richard Loeb?

Unorthodox Broadway producer David Merrick . . .

and unorthodox parent Joel Steinberg?

Movie director Hal Needham . .

and Rev. Jim Jones?

Neglectful husband Claus von Bülow . . .

and accused spy Felix Bloch and . . .

Werner "Colonel Klink" Klemperer?

O

Mel "The Velvet Fog" Tormé . . .

and Jean-Paul "The Existentialist Frog" Sartre?

r, how Lee Majors inspired a generation of prose minimalists.

Literary minimalist Raymond Carver . . .

and minimally literate Lee Majors?

Simon & Schuster publisher Michael Korda . . .

and perpetually struggling comedian Richard Belzer?

Hyperstylish *Vogue* editor Anna Wintour . . .

and hyperstylish author Joan Didion?

Primal scream therapy practitioner Roland Orzabal of *Tears for Fears* . . .

and legendary wit Oscar Wilde?

Impressionistic writer Gabriel García Márquez . . .

and impressionist portrayer Anthony (Gauguin in *Lust for Life*) Quinn?

Cranky editor-publisher
Jason Epstein . . .

and cranky architectural titan
Robert Venturi?

Northern writer
Mordecai Richler . . .

and Southern playwright
Lillian Hellman?

Frowzy mophead Phyllis Diller . . .

and more overwrought frowzy
mophead Barbara Cartland?

Irreverent, erudite Australian
essayist Robert (*The Fatal
Shore*) Hughes . . .

and irreverent, erudite
Anglophilic essayist Paul
(*Wartime*) Fussell?

Trash-novel writer Irwin Shaw . . .

and hash brownie eater Gertrude Stein?

57

Former Python Michael Palin . . .

and former man Jan Morris?

Old Gringo novelist
Carlos Fuentes . . .

and aging gringo comedian
Dan Rowan?

Maurice author E. M. Forster . . .

and *Maude* husband Bill Macy?

Critic Edmund Wilson . . .

and uncritical Cubs skipper
Don Zimmer?

Bloodthirsty author
Gore Vidal . . .

and bloodsucking actor
Frank Langella?

Novelist-cum-politico Mario Vargas Llosa . . .

and Laverne-cum-uteur Penny Marshall?

Young, healthy-scalped Arthur Miller . . .

and young, slender Art Carney?

This Quiet Dust author William Styron . . .

and dusty retired *New York Times* correspondent James Reston?

The Edible Woman author Margaret Atwood . . .

and Agnes Moorehead of *Bewitched?*

Establishment-figure-hater Mary McCarthy . . .

and established figure skater Sonja Henie?

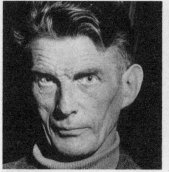

Maverick dramatist Samuel Beckett . . .

and maverick Supreme Court Justice Louis Brandeis . . .

and maverick drummer Ginger Baker?

Ray (*Fahrenheit 451*) Bradbury . . .

and Roger (*At the Movies*) Ebert . . .

and Cynthia (obscure novels you never heard of) Ozick?

ello, city desk? This is Dee

Throat. Get me the host o

Hee Haw—on the double!

Former *New York Times* commandant A. M. Rosenthal . . .

and former *McHale's Navy* captain Joe Flynn?

Suck-up *New York Times* managing editor Arthur Gelb . .

and bloodsucker Dracula?

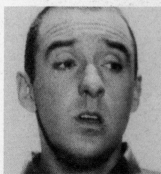

Nightlife legend Carl Bernstein . . .

and *Hee Haw* legend Buck Owens?

Affected hawk William F. Buckley Jr. . . . .

and fake Marine Gomer Pyle?

Patti "Don't Cry for Me Argentina" LuPone . . .

and Judith "Miss Manners" Martin?

Chameleon-like musician Elton John . . .

and *Music for Chameleons* author Truman Capote?

The Bogeyman author George Plimpton . . .

and bogeymanish actor Robert Joy?

Rich architect Philip Johnson . . .

and rich architect-of-a-new-female-sensibility Frances Lear?

Short-tempered screen legend Merle Oberon . . .

and short-sentence gossip columnist Cindy Adams?

Society gossip columnist Suzy . . .

and over-the-top bombshell Anita Morris?

King-of-early-1970s-television Norman Lear . . .

and king-of-early-1970s-baseball Charlie Finley?

Versatile American actor John Lithgow . . .

and *USA Today* gossipeuse Jeannie Williams?

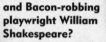

Cradle-robbing designer Mary McFadden . . .

and Bacon-robbing playwright William Shakespeare?

uoth the Bard, "Crushe
velvet is the way to g
this season, and hem
lines will be up, up, up
Now if you'll excuse me,
have to pick up my boy
friend from day care . . . ."

Ostentatiously attractive actor-playwrite Sam Shepard. . .

and career-rebirth celebrant Don Ameche?

Earth mother actress Viveca Lindfors . . .

and *Ur*-defector Rudolf Nureyev?

Pretentious-art-crowd-figurehead-of-his-time Andy Warhol . . .

and pretentious-art-crowd-figurehead-of-*his*-time Alfred Stieglitz?

Brusque character actor Yaphet Kotto . . .

and bruised character actor Oscar Levant?

Seventh Avenue's Calvin Klein . . .

and *West Side Story*'s George Chakiris?

Couture untouchable Yves St. Laurent . . .

and nightmarish movie director David Cronenberg?

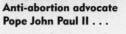

**Anti-abortion advocate
Pope John Paul II . . .**

**and abortion advocate
Molly Yard?**

F

eminism and gonzo journalism, hallowed be thy names.

Tibetan cult figure the Dalai Lama . . .

and college journalism cult figure Hunter S. Thompson?

rankenstein and Fish, walking serenely into the sunset of life together.

Lisp-afflicted Boris Karloff . . .

and Fish-afflicted Abe Vigoda?

Wobbly entertainer George Burns . . .

and entertaining warbler Ella Fitzgerald?

Alabama senator Howell Heflin . . .

and fist-faced actress Anne (*Throw Momma*) Ramsey?

Overpaid decorator Andrée Putman . . .

and rarely played composer John Cage?

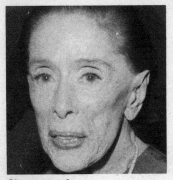

Choreographer
Martha Graham . . .

 74

and the Great Sphinx?

Green Acres proprietor
Eddie Albert . . .

and Oliver North trial judge
Gerhard Gesell?

NBC Sports fixture Vin Scully . . .

Lefty actor Ed Asner . . .

and late night television
commercial fixture
Art Linkletter?

and lefty minister William
Sloane Coffin?

Former Speaker of the House
Carl Albert . . .

and former Rose Marie tag-
along Morey Amsterdam?

Washington fixer
Clark Clifford . . .

and Hollywood fixture
Ralph Bellamy?

Humorist Stan Freberg . . .

and unintentionally
humorous actress Dame
Margaret Rutherford?

Dowdy British figurehead
Queen Elizabeth II. . .

and dowdy brand-name
figurehead Betty Crocker?

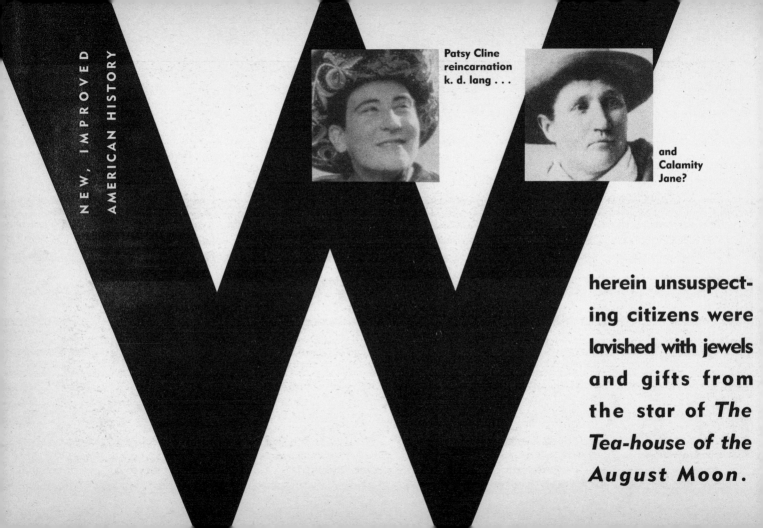

Patsy Cline reincarnation k. d. lang . . .

and Calamity Jane?

**herein unsuspect-
ing citizens were
lavished with jewels
and gifts from
the star of *The
Tea-house of the
August Moon*.**

Ultra-earnest actress
Glenn Close . . .

and ultra-earnest father of our
country George Washington?

Abolitionist John Brown . . .

and *Always* lyricist
Irving Berlin?

Gilda star Glenn Ford . . .

and the Gilded Age's Diamond
Jim Brady?

Vigorous Massachusetts
patriarch Increase Mather . . .

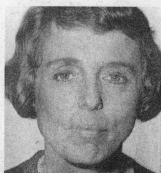

and rigorous *Beverly Hillbillies*
secretary Nancy Kulp?

W

ould that these specimens were in captivity, where they couldn't do us any harm.

Quicker picker-upper Nancy Walker . . .

and Zira from *Planet of the Apes*?

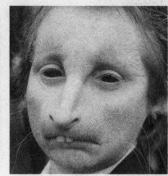

Lucille Ball in *Stone Pillow* . . .

and Ratboy?

ABC News president Roone Arledge . . .

and a giant Galápagos tortoise?

Home-wrecking football has-been Mark Gastineau . . .

and a gorilla?

High-strung has-been Joan Rivers . . .

and high-strung has-been Woody Woodpecker?

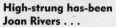

ike we've always said, show business personal-

ities can be so vapid and

. . . well, *two-dimensional*.

Actress Eileen Brennan . . .

and *101 Dalmations* femme fatale Cruella DeVil?

**Old-fashioned TV creation
Dr. Joyce Brothers . . .**

**and Dr. Seuss creation the
Cat in the Hat?**

**Singer and darling-of-WASPs
Bobby Short . . .**

**and bear and darling-of-WASPs
Winnie-the-Pooh?**

**Texas congressman
Henry Gonzalez . . .**

**and *Sesame Street*'s
Fozzie Bear?**

**Animal rights zealot
Betty White . . .**

**and Glinda the Good Witch
from *The Wizard of Oz*?**

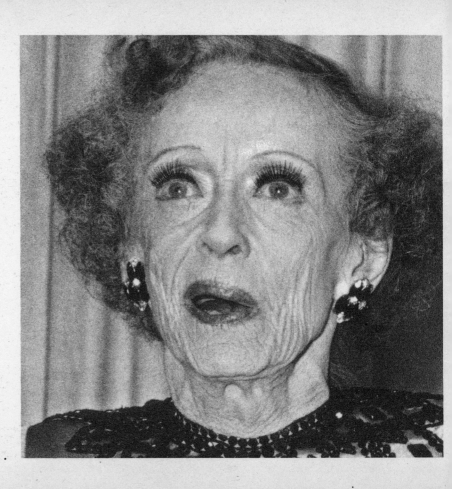

Bette Davis . . .

and the Mean Apple Tree in *The Wizard of Oz*?

A

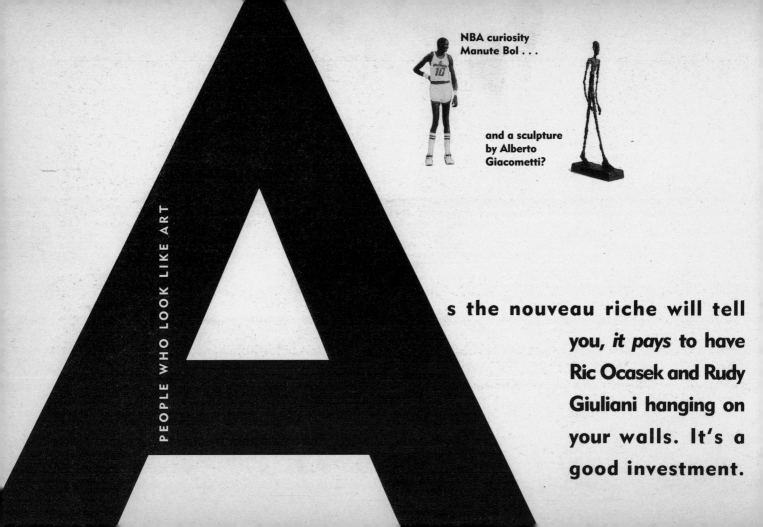

PEOPLE WHO LOOK LIKE ART

NBA curiosity
Manute Bol . . .

and a sculpture
by Alberto
Giacometti?

s the nouveau riche will tell you, *it pays* to have Ric Ocasek and Rudy Giuliani hanging on your walls. It's a good investment.

**Wee critical darling
Linda Hunt . . .**

and a Van Gogh?

**Devoted, hardworking
politician Rudolph Giuliani . . .**

**and the works of devotional
artist Giotto?**

**News curiosity
Sukhreet Gabel . . .**

**and a Fernando Botero
painting?**

**Nepotism poster child
Paloma Picasso . . .**

**and a painting by her dad's
contemporary Fernand Léger?**

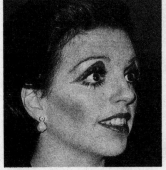

Tacky, waiflike entertainers Liza Minnelli . . .

and Goldie Hawn . . .

and the tacky, waif-depicting drawings of Walter Keane?

Junk-culture diversions Tama Janowitz . . .

and Cher . . .

and the pen-and-ink drawings of Aubrey Beardsley?

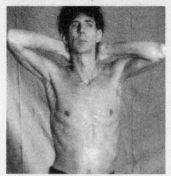

Rock musician toy-boys-of-fashion-models Ric Ocasek . . .

and Keith Richards . . .

and the Expressionist paintings of Egon Schiele?

Ultra-white, cartoonish letter-turner Vanna White . . .

and ultra-cartoonish New York *Daily News* publisher Jim Hoge . . .

and the pop art of Roy Lichtenstein?

N

o wonder Michael Eisner runs Disney. No wonder Leona Helmsley's going to prison. And no wonder Donald Trump gives us the creeps.

Leona Helmsley . . .

and the Joker?

Tall movie magnate Michael Eisner . . .

and *really* tall Disneylandish oddity Andre the Giant?

Hairpiece-wearing defendant Mike Milken . . .

and hairpiece-wearing TV hunk Ted Danson?

Wall Street dabbler Pete Dawkins . . .

and Demon Barber of Fleet Street Len Cariou?

Charlie Watts of the Rolling Stones . . .

and birdseed magnate Leonard Stern?

Australian labor-union-buster Rupert Murdoch . . .

and Israeli Labor Party leader Shimon Peres?

Leveraged-buyout nut Henry Kravis . . .

and Michael Stipe of R.E.M.?

Non-journalist Mort (*U.S. News & World Report*) Zuckerman . . .

and movie director François Truffaut?

Donald Trump . . .

and the Son of Sam police sketch?

Mean Jeane Kirkpatrick... and Iron Mike Tyson?

Joel Grey throws a devastating left hook into Jeane Kirkpatrick's face, and *holy smoke!*—she's down! Separated-at-Birth action—it's FAN-tastic.

Career-milking Vegas attraction Sugar Ray Leonard . . .

and career-milking Vegas attraction Joel Grey?

Base, third-rate movie star Chuck Norris . . .

and third baseman Mike Schmidt?

Exiled Oscar winner F. Murray Abraham . . .

and exiled Yankee manager Yogi Berra?

Chanteuse Josephine Baker . . .

and former NFL commissioner Pete Rozelle?

Underappreciated funnyman
Martin Mull . . .

and overexposed television
gimmick Hulk Hogan?

Tennis brat Jimmy Connors . . .

and talentless brat
Corey Feldman?

Ichabod Crane . . .

and Von Hayes of the Phillies?

Dead baseball character
Billy Martin . . .

and excellent character actor
Harry Dean Stanton?

Celtics forward Larry Bird . . .

and Norwegian marathoner Grete Waitz?

Ex-Senate Majority Leader Robert Byrd . . .

and the St. Louis Cardinals' mascot?

Former Christian Kareem Abdul-Jabbar . . .

and former angry young man Joe Jackson?

French love god Gerard Depardieu . . .

and foul-tempered Slav Ilie Nastase?

R

ockin' with Rushdie and rollin' with Rona.
Plus Mister Rogers doing the samba.

Public television
fixture David Byrne . . .

and public television
fixture Mister Rogers?

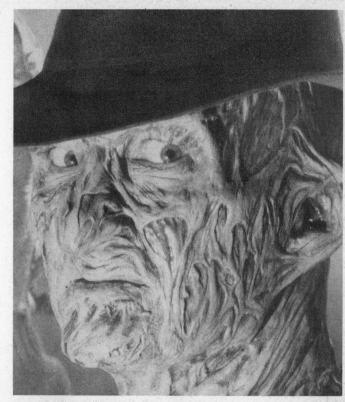

Publicist's nightmare Miles Davis . . .

and manicurist's nightmare Freddy Krueger?

Lounge Lizard John Lurie . . .

and Nick at Nite regular Fred Gwynne?

Around the World in a Day creator Prince . . .

and *Around the World in 80 Days* star Cantinflas?

Gnarly rock poseur Billy Idol . .

and snarly film auteur Jim Jarmusch?

Bad singer Jerry Garcia . . .

and *Mad* publisher William Gaines?

Former journalist Kurt Loder . . .

and former junkie Iggy Pop?

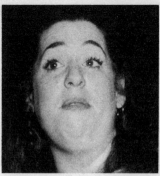

Obstreperous black person Al Sharpton . . .

and ham-sandwich casualty Mama Cass Elliot?

Forcibly retired Morton Downey Jr. . . .

and unretired Mick Jagger?

Arrogant, wooden singer Sting . . .

and arrogant, wood-loving Edgar Bergen?

Dizzy 1970s singer
Stevie Nicks . . .

and 1970s busybody
Rona Barrett?

Reclusive writer
Salman Rushdie . . .

and insufficiently reclusive
drummer Mick Fleetwood?

Right-wing poet Allen Tate . . .

and right-wing musician
Al Jardine of the Beach Boys?

British feminist author
Margaret Drabble . . .

and British 1960s coaster
Peter Noone?

Teenybopper idol Rick Astley . . .

and racetrack novelist Dick Francis?

Sexually ambiguous David Bowie . . .

and shredding enthusiast Fawn Hall?

Mike Tyson sparring partner Mitch Green . . .

and Valerie Simpson marital partner Nick Ashford?

Aging sex enthusiast Rod Stewart . . .

and facial contortionist Charlie Callas?

Hipster Carly Simon . . .

and hoopster Patrick Ewing?

**Simian rock legend
Neil Young . . .**

**and simian comedian
Rich Hall?**

**Unsuccessful studio head
David Puttnam . . .**

**and unsuccessful solo
recording artist John Entwistle?**

Madonna . . .

and *Laugh-In*'s Ruth Buzzi?

Litigious pubescent crooner Tiffany . . .

and ludicrous post-pubescent crooner Julian Lennon?

M

asters of diplomacy, victims of twinning . . . Whatever you do, just don't rush up to Princess Diona in the street and tell her that she looks like Wayne Gretzky. *Bodycheck!*

**Ender of the Cold War
Mikhail Gorbachev . . .**

**and lampooner of the Cold War
Peter Sellers?**

**Gorby television prop
Raisa Gorbachev . . .**

**and gushing television pip
Leeza Gibbons?**

**Heartbeat-away-from-the-
White-House-wife
Marilyn Quayle . . .**

**and heartbeat-away-from-
Buckingham-Palace-husband
Prince Charles?**

**Former disco brat
Princess Diana . . .**

**and Los Angeles King
Wayne Gretzky?**

Pakistani leader Benazir Bhutto . . .

and *SCTV*'s Edith Prickley?

Buddhist convert Richard Gere . . .

and tyro-turned-footnote Fidel Castro?

Costa Rican President Oscar Arias Sánchez . . .

and coasting cartoon character Dondi?

Wonderful actor John Cleese . . .

and Prince Michael of Greece?

Unpleasant dictator Manuel Noriega . . .

and TV comedy legend Bill Dana?

Beloved hoofer Fred Astaire . .

and cloven-hooved former First Nuisance Nancy Reagan?

Jordan's too-cowardly King Hussein . . .

and America's too-brave G. Gordon Liddy?

Shamed, slimy minister Jim Bakker . . .

and Spain's President Felipe Gonzalez?

Difficult mom
Ethel Kennedy . . .

and eternal vaudevillian
Mickey Rooney?

n the unceasing barrage of Kennedy-based miniseries, biographies, memorials, and speculation (all 28 of Joe and Rose's grandchildren will be eligible for House seats by 1999, when 21 of them will be old enough to run for President), there has been little time for any solid scholarly analysis. But at last, a keen observation: *Ethel Kennedy looks just like Mickey Rooney.*

Semiorphaned wealthy person Caroline Kennedy . . .

and orphaned wealth casualty Christina Onassis?

Too-rich, too-thin relic of the early 1960s Lee Radziwill . . .

and gaunt pop artist and relic of the early 1960s Roy Lichtenstein?

Robert F. Kennedy Jr. . . .

and Charlie Chaplin?

Peroxided Hyannis has-been Joan Kennedy . . .

and peroxided Swing Street leftover Peggy Lee?

he President will see you now, Mr. Sununu"; "The President will not see you now, Mr. Hinckley"; "The President will grant you an interview, Mr. Woodward, but before you go in—you didn't also play a black detective on an unsuccessful television show, did you?"

Improbably successful, jumbo-sized chief of staff John Sununu . . .

and improbably successful, jumbo-sized actor John Goodman?

Washington Post star Bob Woodward . . .

and *Sonny Spoon* star Mario Van Peebles?

113

Former U.S. Ambassador to France Evan Galbraith . . .   **and *Batman* star Jack Palance?**

**Right-wing zealot
Newt Gingrich . . .**

**and temperance zealot
Carry Nation?**

**Pugilistic drug czar
William Bennett . . .**

**and nihilistic Giants coach
Bill Parcells?**

**Gun enthusiast and movie buff
Oliver Stone . . .**

**and gun enthusiast and movie
buff John Hinckley?**

***Waltons* grandfather
Will Geer . . .**

**and CIA grandfather
Allen Dulles?**

IF I WERE THE LEADER OF THE FREE WORLD

Men of presidential caliber and their look-alikes. Men like former president Jimmy Carter and former stand-up Garry Shandling.

Quayle-basher Lloyd Bentsen . . .

and a California Rasin?

Mario Cuomo . . .

and Chico Marx?

**Massachusetts irritant
Michael Dukakis . . .**

and MTV irritant Kevin Seal?

**Self-defeatist politician
Jimmy Carter . . .**

**and self-defeatist funnyman
Garry Shandling?**

Loud actor Paul Winfield . . .

**and loud politician
Jesse Jackson?**

Ex-president-for-hire
Gerald Ford . . .

and retro-hero Willy Brandt?

Poindexterish Senator
Paul Simon . . .

and Mr. Peabody from *The Bullwinkle Show?*

Con man chronicler
William Kennedy . . .

and chronic con man
Lyndon LaRouche?

Retired Senator
Howard Baker . . .

and retired NBA coach
Dick Motta?

Slippery character George Wallace . . .

and portrayer-of-slippery-characters Edward G. Robinson?

Lyndon Johnson . . .

and director William Wyler?

Onetime-employee-of-a-grade-B-western-actor Al Haig . . .

and grade-B western actor Cameron Mitchell?

Tiresome Democratic congressman Dick Gephardt . . .

and perpetually tired-looking actress Sissy Spacek?

George Bush . . .

and Reagan EPA
Director William
Ruckelshaus?

George and Brent. George and the two Williams. George and Donald and Nicholas. The upshot is clear: all well-fed middle-aged Republicans in dark suits bear a striking resemblance to their boss.

George Bush . . .

and National Security Adviser
Brent Scowcroft?

George Bush . . .

and Secretary of the Treasury
Nicholas Brady?

George Bush . . .

and CIA Director
William Webster?

George Bush . . .

and former Secretary of
Defense Donald Rumsfeld?

INDEX

PHOTO CREDITS

YOU'VE READ THE BOOK. NOW READ THE MAGAZINE.

GET *SPY* EVERY MONTH.

SUBSCRIBE TO  NOW!

For just $19.95 — 44% off the cover price — you'll get 12 issues of SPY.

In every issue, month after month,

you'll get brand-new "Separated at Birth?" pairs.

PLUS
a sly, satirical take on events of the day.

PLUS
the most acerbic inside dope published anywhere in America.

PLUS
provocative features on everything from the power elite

to glamour surgery to Hollywood feuds.

PLUS
smart cartoons and terrifying facts and the world's only humorous crossword puzzle.

JOIN IN THE FUN. GET *SPY*.